INTRODUCTION

In a world where diversity is celebrated and individuality is cherished, the journey of self-discovery is a transformative experience. Each person possesses a unique set of colors that make them who they are, and one aspect that holds tremendous significance in this tapestry of identity is sexual orientation. Exploring and understanding one's own sexual orientation is a deeply personal and courageous endeavor, but sharing this truth with family and friends can be both exhilarating and daunting.

"Embracing My True Colors: A Guide to Explaining Your Sexual Orientation to Family and Friends" is a compass to navigate the complex landscape of self-disclosure, providing invaluable support and guidance for individuals embarking on this heartfelt journey. Whether you identify as lesbian, gay, bisexual, transgender, queer, or any other part of the beautifully diverse spectrum of sexual orientations, this book is a resource designed to empower you as you traverse the uncharted waters of coming out.

Coming out, in its essence, is an act of self-liberation and an affirmation of authenticity. It is a proclamation of love, trust, and vulnerability, where individuals open the doors to their true selves and invite others to witness their innermost truths. However, this deeply personal revelation is not without its challenges. Fears of rejection, misunderstanding, or alienation may cloud the path, making it difficult to find the right words, time, and approach to share this integral part of who you are with those you love.

With "Embracing My True Colors," we aim to provide you with a roadmap for these pivotal conversations, helping you navigate the emotional terrains and facilitating healthy and constructive dialogue with your family and friends. This guide is not about changing minds or seeking approval; instead, it is about fostering understanding, empathy, and acceptance through open and honest communication.

Drawing from the experiences of individuals who have embarked on similar journeys, as well as insights from mental health professionals, this book offers practical advice, compassionate guidance, and thoughtful strategies to help you articulate your sexual orientation in a way that honors your truth while fostering understanding among your loved ones. It covers a wide range of topics, including preparing for the conversation, choosing the right time and place, addressing common concerns, dispelling myths, and providing resources for continued support.

"Embracing My True Colors" aims to uplift and empower you as you embark on this transformative chapter of your life. Remember, you are not alone on this path. There is a community of individuals who have stood in your shoes, faced similar challenges, and emerged stronger and more authentic than ever before. Through the pages of this book, we hope to be your steadfast companion, offering encouragement, wisdom, and practical tools to help you navigate the sometimes turbulent, but ultimately rewarding, process of sharing your true colors with those who matter most.

So, take a deep breath, summon your courage, and prepare to embark on a journey of self-discovery, authenticity, and love. Your true colors deserve to be celebrated, and together, we will navigate the waters of understanding, compassion, and acceptance, paving the way for a future where every individual is embraced for who they truly are.

CHAPTER 1: UNDERSTANDING YOUR SEXUAL ORIENTATION

Sexual orientation is an integral part of human identity and refers to an individual's enduring pattern of emotional, romantic, and/or sexual attractions to individuals of the same or different gender. It plays a significant role in shaping relationships, self-perception, and overall well-being. Understanding and embracing your sexual orientation is a journey that involves self-reflection, exploration, and self-acceptance. In this chapter, we will define sexual orientation, explore the spectrum of sexual orientations, reflect on personal experiences and feelings, and recognize the importance of self-acceptance.

Defining Sexual Orientation

Sexual orientation is a deeply personal and individual aspect of identity that encompasses a range of attractions and desires. It is important to note that sexual orientation is distinct from gender identity, which relates to one's internal sense of being male, female, or something else.

The most commonly recognized sexual orientations are heterosexual, homosexual, and bisexual. Heterosexual individuals experience attractions to people of the opposite gender, homosexual individuals experience attractions to people of the same gender, and bisexual individuals experience attractions to people of both the same and opposite genders.

However, it is essential to recognize that sexual orientation exists on a spectrum, and there are numerous other orientations beyond these three. Some individuals may identify as pansexual, experiencing attractions regardless of gender, while others may identify as asexual, experiencing little to no sexual attraction. There are also individuals who identify as queer or questioning, as they may be exploring their attractions and have not yet defined a specific orientation.

Exploring The Spectrum Of Sexual Orientations

The spectrum of sexual orientations is vast and diverse, highlighting the complexity of human sexuality. Here are some additional sexual orientations to consider:

Pansexual: Pansexual individuals are attracted to people regardless of their gender identity or biological sex. They value emotional and physical connections based on personal qualities rather than gender.

Asexual: Asexual individuals experience little to no sexual attraction. They may still experience romantic or emotional attractions and can form fulfilling relationships without a strong emphasis on sexual activity.

Demisexual: Demisexual individuals typically experience sexual attraction only after forming a strong emotional bond with someone. They often require a deep connection or emotional intimacy before experiencing sexual desire.

Polysexual: Polysexual individuals are attracted to multiple genders but not necessarily all genders. They may be attracted to some genders while not experiencing attraction to others.

Queer: The term "queer" is often used as an

umbrella term to encompass a wide range of non-heterosexual orientations. It can be embraced by individuals who feel that other labels do not fully capture their experiences or who are still exploring their sexual orientation.

Reflecting On Personal Experiences And Feelings

Exploring your sexual orientation is a deeply personal and introspective process. It involves reflecting on your experiences, feelings, and attractions. Here are some questions to consider:

Who have you been attracted to throughout your life?

Have these attractions been limited to a specific gender or varied across the spectrum?

How do you feel when you imagine yourself in a romantic or sexual relationship with someone of the same gender?

What about someone of a different gender?

Have you ever felt a strong emotional or romantic connection with someone without feeling a strong sexual attraction?

Or have you experienced sexual desire only after forming a close emotional bond with someone?

How do you feel about the idea of being in

a relationship with someone who does not fit traditional gender expectations?

Reflecting on these questions can provide insight into your own sexual orientation. It's important to remember that sexual orientation can be fluid and may change or evolve over time. The most important aspect is to be true to yourself and embrace your feelings and attractions without judgment.

Recognizing The Importance Of Self-Acceptance

Understanding and accepting your sexual orientation is a crucial step towards overall well-being and self-fulfillment. Here are some reasons why self-acceptance is essential:

Authenticity: Embracing your sexual orientation allows you to live authentically and be true to yourself. Denying or suppressing your feelings can lead to internal conflicts and a sense of dissatisfaction.

Emotional Well-being: Self-acceptance promotes emotional well-being by reducing stress, anxiety, and depression related to hiding or denying your sexual orientation. It allows you to cultivate healthy relationships based on openness and honesty.

Building Supportive Networks: Accepting your

sexual orientation empowers you to seek out and connect with supportive communities and networks of individuals who share similar experiences. These networks can provide understanding, acceptance, and guidance during your journey.

Education and Advocacy: By accepting and embracing your sexual orientation, you can become an advocate for yourself and others. Sharing your experiences and educating others about the diversity of sexual orientations helps create a more inclusive and accepting society.

Understanding your sexual orientation is a deeply personal journey that involves self-reflection, exploration, and self-acceptance. Sexual orientation exists on a spectrum, and there are numerous orientations beyond the commonly recognized heterosexual, homosexual, and bisexual categories. By reflecting on personal experiences and feelings, individuals can gain insight into their sexual orientation and make strides towards self-acceptance. Remember, embracing your sexual orientation is an essential step towards living authentically and fostering personal well-being.

CHAPTER 2: PREPARING FOR THE CONVERSATION

Assessing Your Readiness

Coming out and explaining your sexual orientation to family and friends can be an emotional and challenging experience. It's important to take the time to assess your readiness before having these conversations. Here are some key factors to consider:

Self-Acceptance: Before opening up to others, it's crucial to have a strong sense of self-acceptance and understanding of your own sexual orientation. Take the time to reflect on your feelings and emotions, and ensure that you are comfortable with your identity.

Education and Awareness: Familiarize yourself with different aspects of sexual orientation, including common misconceptions, societal attitudes, and relevant terminology. This knowledge will empower you to have informed discussions and address any misconceptions or stereotypes that may arise.

Stability and Independence: Assess your current living situation and financial independence. If you are financially dependent on your family or living in an environment that may not be supportive, it may be wise to delay the conversation until you have a more secure foundation.

Setting Realistic Expectations

When preparing for conversations about your sexual orientation, it's essential to establish realistic expectations. Remember that everyone's journey is unique, and reactions can vary widely. Here are some points to consider:

Personal Growth: Understand that coming out is a process, both for you and your loved ones. It may take time for them to fully comprehend and accept your sexual orientation. Be patient and allow for their own personal growth and understanding.

Diverse Reactions: People may react differently

based on their individual beliefs, experiences, and cultural backgrounds. While some may be accepting and supportive from the beginning, others may struggle with understanding or acceptance. Be prepared for a range of reactions and try to approach each conversation with an open mind.

Time and Perspective: Remember that it may take time for your family and friends to adjust to the new information. Initially, they may have questions or concerns, but with time and open communication, they might come to a place of acceptance and support.

Finding Support Systems

Building a support system is crucial during this time. Having individuals who understand and validate your experiences can provide emotional strength and guidance. Consider these avenues for support:

Friends and Peers: Seek out friends or peers who are supportive and understanding. They may have gone through similar experiences and can provide advice, empathy, and encouragement.

LGBTQ+ Communities: Join LGBTQ+ support groups, either in person or online. These communities can offer a sense of belonging, validation, and resources to help you navigate your coming-out journey.

Professional Help: If needed, consider seeking guidance from mental health professionals, such as therapists or counselors, who specialize in LGBTQ+ issues. They can provide a safe space to explore your feelings and offer strategies for coping with any challenges that may arise.

Building Emotional Resilience

Preparing emotionally for these conversations is vital to navigate any potential challenges or negative reactions. Here are some strategies to build emotional resilience:

Self-Care: Prioritize self-care activities that promote your well-being, such as exercise, meditation, journaling, or engaging in hobbies you enjoy. Taking care of yourself physically and mentally will help you manage stress and maintain emotional balance.

Education and Advocacy: Educate yourself about LGBTQ+ history, rights, and achievements. This knowledge can empower you and provide a sense of pride and resilience as you navigate conversations with your loved ones.

Assertive Communication: Practice assertive communication skills to express your thoughts, feelings, and needs clearly and respectfully. This can help you navigate difficult conversations and set boundaries if necessary.

Positive Affirmations: Develop positive affirmations that reinforce your self-worth and identity. Repeat them daily to build confidence and resilience in the face of potential challenges or negative reactions.

Practice Empathy: Remember that coming out can also be a transformative experience for your loved ones. Practice empathy by considering their perspectives and fears. This can help you approach conversations with compassion and understanding.

Preparing for conversations about your sexual orientation requires careful self-assessment, setting realistic expectations, finding support systems, and building emotional resilience. By taking these steps, you will be better equipped to navigate the challenges that may arise and have more meaningful and authentic conversations with your family and friends. Remember that embracing your true colors is a journey, and each step forward is an opportunity for growth and self-acceptance.

CHAPTER 3: CHOOSING THE RIGHT TIMING AND SETTING

Evaluating The Dynamics Of Your Relationships

When it comes to discussing your sexual orientation with family and friends, it's essential to evaluate the dynamics of your relationships. Each relationship is unique, and the level of acceptance and understanding may vary. Consider the following factors:

Trust and Openness: Assess the level of trust and openness in your relationship with each person. Are they generally supportive and accepting? Have you had open conversations about personal matters in the past? If you feel comfortable discussing sensitive topics with them, it may indicate a positive dynamic.

Previous Reactions: Reflect on any previous reactions from your family or friends regarding LGBTQ+ topics. If they have shown support, empathy, or an open-minded attitude, it might indicate a higher likelihood of acceptance. Conversely, if they have expressed prejudices or negative views, you may need to approach the conversation more cautiously.

Communication Styles: Consider the communication styles of your loved ones. Do they typically engage in open, honest, and respectful conversations? Are they receptive to differing opinions? Understanding their communication patterns can help you prepare for the discussion and anticipate their reactions.

Identifying An Appropriate Time And Place For The Conversation

Choosing the right time and place for the conversation is crucial to ensure a comfortable and productive dialogue. Here are some considerations to keep in mind:

Privacy and Confidentiality: Find a setting that allows for privacy and confidentiality. This will enable you to have an open and honest conversation without interruptions or distractions. It's essential to create a safe space where everyone involved can express themselves freely.

Relaxed Atmosphere: Select a time and place where everyone is likely to be relaxed and open-minded. Avoid initiating the conversation during stressful periods, such as family gatherings or when tensions are already high. Instead, choose a time when everyone is in a calm and receptive state of mind.

Sufficient Time: Plan the conversation when you have enough time to talk without feeling rushed or pressured. It's crucial to allow for an open dialogue and give your loved ones an opportunity to ask questions or express their thoughts and emotions.

Creating A Comfortable And Safe Environment

To ensure a comfortable and safe environment during the discussion, consider the following steps:

Openness and Vulnerability: Begin the conversation by expressing your genuine feelings and vulnerability. Let your loved ones know that you trust them enough to share this aspect of your life and that you value their support and understanding.

Active Listening: Encourage open dialogue by actively listening to your family and friends' responses and concerns. Provide them with the opportunity to express their thoughts, emotions, and ask questions. Show empathy and understanding, even if their initial reactions are not what you had hoped for.

Setting Boundaries: Establish boundaries to ensure the conversation remains respectful and constructive. Make it clear that derogatory language, discriminatory comments, or personal attacks will not be tolerated. Setting these boundaries can help maintain a healthy and productive conversation.

Considering Cultural And Religious Factors

Cultural and religious factors can significantly influence how individuals perceive and respond to discussions about sexual orientation. Consider the following strategies when navigating these aspects:

Research and Education: Familiarize yourself with the cultural and religious beliefs that may impact your loved ones' perspectives. Educate yourself about their traditions, values, and teachings regarding sexual orientation. This will help you anticipate potential concerns and respond with empathy and understanding.

Personal Testimony: Share your personal experiences and emotions to bridge the gap between your loved ones' cultural or religious beliefs and your sexual orientation. By demonstrating your sincerity and allowing them to empathize with your journey, you may increase the likelihood of them being open to understanding your perspective.

Seek Supportive Resources: Look for resources that align with your loved ones' cultural or religious background and promote acceptance of LGBTQ+ individuals. Books, articles, or community organizations that provide a compassionate and inclusive perspective can be helpful in fostering understanding.

Choosing the right timing and setting for discussing your sexual orientation with family and friends is crucial for creating a comfortable and safe environment. Evaluating the dynamics of your relationships, identifying an appropriate time and place, and considering cultural and religious factors can contribute to a more productive and understanding conversation. Remember, every situation is unique, and it's essential to approach the discussion with empathy, patience, and an open mind.

CHAPTER 4: FRAMING YOUR STORY

Crafting Your Narrative

When it comes to explaining your sexual orientation to family and friends, crafting your narrative is an essential step in effectively communicating your truth. Your narrative is the story you choose to share, the words you use, and the way you express your experiences and emotions. Here are some important considerations to keep in mind as you craft your story:

Self-reflection: Before you begin crafting your narrative, take some time for self-reflection. Understand your own journey, experiences, and emotions surrounding your sexual orientation. This self-awareness will help you articulate your story more effectively and confidently.

Decide on your message: Think about the main message you want to convey to your loved ones. Is it about self-acceptance, the importance of understanding and support, or simply sharing your truth? Having a clear message in mind will help you stay focused while crafting your narrative.

Choose the right time and place: Find a suitable setting where you can have an uninterrupted conversation with your family or friends. Consider the emotional state of the individuals you're speaking to and choose a time when they are more likely to be receptive and open-minded.

Be authentic: Authenticity is key when sharing your story. Speak from the heart and use language that reflects your true feelings. People are more likely to connect with your story when they can sense your sincerity.

Exploring Different Communication Styles

Not everyone communicates in the same way, and it's important to consider the individual communication styles of your family and friends. Here are some common styles you may encounter and tips for navigating them:

Direct communicators: These individuals prefer clear and concise communication. They appreciate honesty and straightforwardness. When speaking to direct communicators, be clear and concise in explaining your sexual orientation. Provide them with factual information and address any questions or concerns they may have.

Indirect communicators: Indirect communicators often rely on subtle cues and hints. They may find direct discussions uncomfortable or confrontational. With indirect communicators, it can be helpful to start the conversation by sharing your emotions and experiences without explicitly mentioning your sexual orientation. Allow them to connect the dots themselves and create a safe space for them to ask questions.

Visual learners: Some individuals learn and understand better through visual aids. Consider creating a visual presentation or using diagrams, charts, or videos to help explain your sexual orientation. Visual learners may find it easier to process information when it's presented visually.

Addressing Fears And Concerns

Sharing your sexual orientation can evoke various fears and concerns from your family and friends. It's essential to address these anxieties with empathy and understanding. Here are some common fears and concerns and tips for addressing them:

Fear of the unknown: Many people fear what they do not understand. Assure your loved ones that your sexual orientation is not a choice, and it is a natural aspect of who you are. Provide them with resources, such as books, articles, or support groups, that can help them educate themselves and overcome their fear of the unknown.

Concerns about societal judgment: Society's attitudes and prejudices can be a source of concern for both you and your loved ones. Address these concerns by emphasizing the importance of love, acceptance, and inclusivity. Share stories of acceptance and positive experiences from the LGBTQ+ community to help alleviate their worries about societal judgment.

Worries about family dynamics: Family dynamics can be deeply rooted, and some individuals may worry that your sexual orientation will disrupt family relationships. Reassure them that your sexual orientation does not change who you are as a person or your love for them. Emphasize the importance of maintaining open and honest communication to strengthen family bonds.

Balancing Honesty And Sensitivity

Finding the right balance between honesty and sensitivity is crucial when explaining your sexual orientation. While it's important to be truthful about your experiences and emotions, it's equally vital to be sensitive to the reactions and emotions of your loved ones. Here are some tips for achieving this balance:

Use "I" statements: Frame your narrative using "I" statements to express your personal experiences and feelings. This helps avoid sounding accusatory or confrontational and allows your loved ones to understand your perspective without feeling attacked.

Validate their emotions: Understand that your loved ones may experience a range of emotions when you share your sexual orientation. Validate their feelings and let them know that you understand their initial surprise, confusion, or concern. Reassure them that it is natural to have questions and that you are open to discussing their feelings further.

Offer support and resources: Make it clear to your loved ones that you are available to provide support and answer any questions they may have. Offer resources such as LGBTQ+ organizations, books, or online communities that can help them further educate themselves and find support from others who have gone through similar experiences.

Crafting your narrative is a pivotal step in explaining your sexual orientation to family and friends. By reflecting on your journey, understanding your audience's communication styles, addressing fears and concerns, and balancing honesty with sensitivity, you can effectively communicate your truth. Remember, sharing your sexual orientation is a personal decision, and it's important to prioritize your emotional well-being throughout the process.

CHAPTER 5: NAVIGATING REACTIONS AND RESPONSES

Understanding Potential Reactions From Family And Friends

When you decide to come out and explain your sexual orientation to your family and friends, it's important to understand that their reactions may vary widely. Some individuals may respond with acceptance, support, and love, while others may struggle with confusion, rejection, or even ignorance. Being prepared for these potential reactions can help you navigate the process with more ease and resilience.

Acceptance and Support: Fortunately, many people

find that their loved ones respond with acceptance and support. They may express their love for you, affirm your identity, and reassure you of their unwavering support. This positive response can strengthen your relationships and create an environment of love and understanding.

Confusion and Uncertainty: Some individuals may not have prior knowledge or experience with different sexual orientations, and your disclosure may leave them feeling confused or uncertain. They might struggle to comprehend the concept, have limited exposure to diverse sexual orientations, or hold preconceived notions based on societal stereotypes. It's essential to approach their confusion with patience, empathy, and a willingness to educate them.

Rejection and Disapproval: Unfortunately, not everyone will respond positively to your coming out. Rejection and disapproval can stem from deeply ingrained beliefs, cultural or religious biases, fear of the unknown, or a lack of understanding. It can be challenging to face rejection from those you love, but remember that their reactions are not a reflection of your worth or validity. It's important to prioritize your mental and emotional well-being, seeking support from understanding friends or LGBTQ+ support groups.

Denial and Ignorance: Some individuals may respond to your disclosure with denial or ignorance, refusing to acknowledge or accept your sexual orientation. They might attempt to invalidate your identity, dismiss your feelings, or even attribute your orientation to a phase or confusion. It's important to remember that their denial or ignorance is a reflection of their own limitations and not a reflection of your truth. It's crucial to set boundaries and prioritize your own well-being when faced with these reactions.

Dealing With Rejection, Confusion, Or Ignorance

Encountering rejection, confusion, or ignorance from family and friends can be challenging and emotionally draining. Here are some strategies to help you navigate these reactions:

Process Your Feelings: Allow yourself to experience and process the emotions that come with these reactions. It's normal to feel hurt, disappointed, or angry. Find healthy outlets for your emotions, such as talking to a trusted friend, journaling, or seeking therapy. Remember to prioritize self-care during this time.

Seek Support: Reach out to friends, supportive family members, or LGBTQ+ support groups for emotional support. Surrounding yourself with individuals who validate and affirm your identity can help counteract the negative impact of rejection or ignorance. They can provide a safe space for you to express your feelings and offer guidance based on their own experiences.

Educate and Inform: For those who respond with confusion or ignorance, consider educating them about sexual orientation and providing resources that can help them understand better. Share articles, books, documentaries, or online resources that explain various sexual orientations and address common misconceptions. Encourage them to approach the topic with an open mind and engage in respectful dialogue.

Set Boundaries: If you encounter persistent rejection or negativity from certain individuals, it's crucial to set boundaries to protect your well-being. Communicate your needs clearly and assertively, expressing that their harmful reactions are not acceptable. This might involve limiting contact, taking a break from the relationship, or establishing clear expectations for respectful communication.

Focus on Acceptance: While it can be disheartening to experience rejection or ignorance, it's important to remember that you deserve acceptance and love. Surround yourself with individuals who embrace and affirm your identity. Celebrate and prioritize relationships that support your well-being and foster a sense of belonging.

Responding To Questions And Misconceptions

When faced with questions or misconceptions about your sexual orientation, it's essential to approach the situation with patience, empathy, and a willingness to educate. Here are some tips for responding effectively:

Stay Calm and Composed: Keep your emotions in check when responding to questions or misconceptions. Staying calm can help maintain a productive conversation and prevent misunderstandings or unnecessary conflicts. Take deep breaths and remember that educating others is an opportunity for growth and understanding.

Be Open and Honest: Respond to questions and misconceptions honestly, using your own experiences and knowledge. Share personal stories or anecdotes that can help the person relate to your perspective. Emphasize that sexual orientation is a deeply personal aspect of one's identity and cannot be changed or influenced.

Provide Resources: Offer books, articles, documentaries, or websites that provide accurate and reliable information on sexual orientation. Sharing credible resources can help dispel misconceptions and allow the person to explore the topic further on their own. Encourage them to educate themselves and approach the subject with an open mind.

Correct Misconceptions: If someone holds misconceptions or stereotypes about your sexual orientation, kindly correct them. Provide accurate information and challenge their assumptions respectfully. Remember that change takes time, and it may require multiple conversations or exposure to different perspectives for misconceptions to be fully addressed.

Empathy and Understanding: Recognize that individuals may struggle to understand or accept your sexual orientation due to their own upbringing, beliefs, or lack of exposure to diverse identities. Approach their questions or misconceptions with empathy, understanding that they might be grappling with internal conflicts or fear of the unknown. Foster an environment of open dialogue, encouraging them to ask further questions and learn more.

Encouraging Open Dialogue And Understanding

Creating an atmosphere of open dialogue and understanding can foster acceptance and facilitate productive conversations about sexual orientation. Here are some strategies to encourage such an environment:

Lead by Example: Be open about your own sexual orientation, sharing your experiences and feelings. By being authentic and vulnerable, you can inspire others to approach the topic with openness and curiosity.

Normalize Discussions: Encourage discussions about sexual orientation in a natural and non-judgmental manner. Share articles, news stories, or current events related to LGBTQ+ topics to promote dialogue and understanding. Be open to answering questions and providing information when people show an interest.

Active Listening: Practice active listening when engaging in conversations about sexual orientation. Give others the space to express their thoughts, emotions, and concerns. Validate their feelings and experiences, even if they don't align with your own. This can help create a safe and respectful environment for open dialogue.

Respectful Communication: Set ground rules for respectful communication within your social circles. Encourage everyone to express their opinions and ask questions without resorting to insults, judgments, or personal attacks. Emphasize the importance of mutual respect and empathy when discussing sensitive topics.

Patience and Persistence: Remember that change takes time. Some individuals may need more exposure, education, or personal growth to fully understand and accept diverse sexual orientations. Be patient and persistent in your efforts to foster understanding, knowing that small steps can lead to significant transformations.

Navigating reactions and responses when explaining your sexual orientation to family and friends can be both empowering and challenging. While some individuals may respond with acceptance and support, others may struggle with confusion, rejection, or ignorance. By understanding potential reactions, managing your own emotions, and responding with empathy and education, you can foster a more inclusive and understanding environment. Remember to prioritize your own well-being, seek support from understanding individuals, and celebrate the relationships that embrace and affirm your true colors.

CHAPTER 6: OVERCOMING CHALLENGES

Managing Emotional Setbacks

Exploring and understanding your sexual orientation can be a deeply personal and emotional journey. As you come out to your family and friends, it's important to be prepared for potential emotional setbacks. Not everyone may react positively or accept your sexual orientation immediately, and that can be challenging to navigate. Here are some strategies to help you manage emotional setbacks effectively:

Give Yourself Time: Coming to terms with your sexual orientation is a process that takes time, and the same goes for your loved ones. Understand that their reactions may not reflect their true feelings in the long run. Allow yourself the space to process your emotions and give them time to do the same.

Practice Self-Care: Taking care of your emotional well-being is crucial during challenging times. Engage in activities that bring you joy, such as hobbies, exercise, or spending time with supportive friends. Make sure to prioritize self-care to maintain a positive mindset and overall emotional health.

Seek Support: Reach out to friends or family members who are accepting and supportive of your sexual orientation. Having a strong support system can help alleviate feelings of isolation and provide a safe space for you to express your emotions. Online communities and LGBTQ+ support groups can also offer valuable support and understanding.

Express Your Feelings: It's essential to express your emotions and not bottle them up. Find healthy outlets to vent, such as journaling, talking to a trusted friend, or seeking therapy. Acknowledging and processing your feelings can prevent them from overwhelming you in the long run.

Handling Judgment And Discrimination

Unfortunately, judgment and discrimination are realities that some individuals face when coming out. Dealing with these challenges can be disheartening, but remember that you are not alone. Here are some strategies to help you handle judgment and discrimination:

Educate Yourself: Educating yourself about LGBTQ + rights, history, and legal protections can empower you to navigate discrimination effectively. Understanding your rights and knowing the resources available to you can make a significant difference in advocating for yourself and seeking appropriate support.

Stay Safe: Prioritize your safety above all else. If you find yourself in a situation where you feel threatened or unsafe, remove yourself from it and seek help from a trusted individual or authority figure. Your safety should always be the top priority.

Set Boundaries: It's important to establish boundaries with individuals who exhibit judgmental or discriminatory behavior. Clearly communicate your expectations and let them know that derogatory comments or mistreatment will not be tolerated. If necessary, distance yourself from toxic relationships that are detrimental to your well-being.

Build a Support Network: Surround yourself with people who accept and support you unconditionally. Seek out LGBTQ+ organizations, support groups, or online communities where you can connect with like-minded individuals who can provide guidance and empathy. Building a strong support network can help you navigate difficult situations and provide a sense of belonging.

Seeking Professional Support If Needed

If you find that emotional setbacks, judgment, or discrimination are taking a toll on your mental health, seeking professional support can be incredibly beneficial. Therapists who specialize in LGBTQ+ issues can provide a safe and nonjudgmental space for you to express your feelings and work through the challenges you're facing. A trained professional can offer guidance, coping strategies, and help you build resilience during this time.

Building Resilience And Self-Confidence

Building resilience and self-confidence is essential for navigating the challenges that may arise when coming out to family and friends. Here are some strategies to help you strengthen your resilience and embrace your true colors:

Practice Self-Affirmation: Remind yourself of your worth and the importance of embracing your sexual orientation. Write down positive affirmations and repeat them daily to boost your self-confidence. Affirmations can help counter negative thoughts and reinforce your self-acceptance.

Surround Yourself with Positivity: Surrounding yourself with positive influences can significantly impact your self-confidence. Seek out role models, stories, and media that celebrate diverse sexual orientations. Engaging with affirming content can help you build resilience and foster a sense of belonging.

Celebrate Your Identity: Embrace and celebrate your sexual orientation as an integral part of your identity. Participate in LGBTQ+ events, join advocacy groups, or contribute to LGBTQ+ causes. Engaging in activities that celebrate your identity can boost your self-confidence and provide a sense of community.

Educate Others: Sharing your story and educating others about sexual orientation can be empowering. By dispelling myths and misconceptions, you can contribute to creating a more accepting and inclusive environment. Advocacy and education not only help others understand, but they also reinforce your own self-confidence and resilience.

Overcoming challenges when coming out to family and friends requires emotional strength, resilience, and self-confidence. By managing emotional setbacks, handling judgment and discrimination, seeking professional support when needed, and building resilience, you can navigate this journey more effectively. Remember that your true colors are beautiful, and you have the right to live authentically and be proud of who you are. Embrace your journey, and know that there is a community of support waiting to welcome you with open arms.

CHAPTER 7: EMBRACING ACCEPTANCE AND UNDERSTANDING

Cultivating Empathy And Patience

When it comes to explaining your sexual orientation to family and friends, cultivating empathy and patience is crucial. It's important to remember that their reactions may vary, and not everyone will immediately understand or accept your truth. Here are some strategies for cultivating empathy and patience throughout the process:

Put yourself in their shoes: Try to understand the perspectives and beliefs of your loved ones.

Remember that their reactions may be influenced by their upbringing, cultural background, or personal experiences. By empathizing with their point of view, you can approach the conversation with more understanding and compassion.

Communicate openly and honestly: Create an open and safe space for dialogue. Encourage your family and friends to share their thoughts and feelings. This open communication can help bridge the gap and foster understanding on both sides.

Practice active listening: Pay attention to what your loved ones are saying, both verbally and non-verbally. Listen without interrupting or judging. Reflecting back on what they've said can demonstrate that you value their perspective and are willing to engage in a respectful conversation.

Show patience: Understand that acceptance takes time. It may take your loved ones a while to process the information and adjust their beliefs. Be patient and give them the space they need to come to terms with your sexual orientation.

Celebrating Small Victories And Milestones

Throughout your journey of explaining your sexual orientation, it's important to celebrate the small victories and milestones along the way. These moments can provide a sense of encouragement and affirmation. Here are some ways to celebrate these achievements:

Acknowledge progress: Recognize the progress made in your relationships with family and friends. Whether it's a small shift in their understanding or an acceptance of your identity, celebrate these positive steps forward.

Share milestones with trusted allies: Surround yourself with a support system that understands and accepts you. Share your milestones with them and let them join in the celebration. Their encouragement and validation can boost your confidence and resilience.

Reflect on personal growth: Take the time to reflect on your own personal growth and journey. Recognize the strength and courage it takes to be true to yourself and navigate these conversations. Acknowledge how far you've come and celebrate the person you've become.

Encouraging Education And Awareness

One effective way to foster acceptance and understanding among your family and friends is through education and awareness. By providing them with information about sexual orientation and LGBTQ+ issues, you can help dispel misconceptions and promote a more inclusive environment. Here's how you can encourage education and awareness:

Share reliable resources: Share books, articles, documentaries, or websites that provide accurate and comprehensive information about sexual orientation. Choose resources that are accessible and resonate with your loved ones' interests and learning styles.

Recommend LGBTQ+ organizations: Introduce your family and friends to LGBTQ+ organizations and support groups. These organizations often offer educational materials and resources designed to promote understanding and acceptance.

Encourage open dialogue: Facilitate discussions where your loved ones can ask questions and express their concerns in a safe and non-judgmental environment. Encourage them to challenge their preconceived notions and biases.

Lead by example: Be open about your own learning journey and share the knowledge you've gained. Demonstrate a willingness to engage in ongoing education and growth, which can inspire others to do the same.

Fostering A Supportive And Inclusive Environment

Creating a supportive and inclusive environment is essential for your own well-being and for the growth of your relationships with family and friends. Here are some strategies to foster such an environment:

Set boundaries: Establish clear boundaries for what is acceptable and respectful behavior. Communicate these boundaries to your loved ones and hold them accountable. This will help create a safe space where you can be open about your sexual orientation without fear of judgment or discrimination.

Seek allies: Identify individuals within your family or friend circle who are supportive and accepting. Foster relationships with these allies and lean on them for support during difficult times.

Their presence can provide a source of strength and encouragement.

Create opportunities for exposure: Invite your family and friends to LGBTQ+ events, pride parades, or community gatherings. Exposing them to diverse experiences can challenge stereotypes and promote understanding.

Be patient with resistance: Understand that resistance or discomfort may arise from your loved ones as they adjust to your sexual orientation. Respond with patience and empathy, giving them time to process and grow. Remember, change often takes time, and your understanding can help facilitate that process.

Embracing acceptance and understanding when

explaining your sexual orientation to family and friends requires cultivating empathy, patience, and open communication. Celebrating small victories and milestones can provide encouragement and motivation throughout the process. Encouraging education and awareness about sexual orientation and fostering a supportive and inclusive environment are essential for long-term acceptance and understanding. Remember that each person's journey is unique, and with time, love, and understanding, relationships can grow stronger and more authentic.

CHAPTER 8: REBUILDING RELATIONSHIPS

Healing strained relationships, especially when it comes to explaining your sexual orientation to family and friends, can be a challenging and emotional process. However, with patience, understanding, and effective communication, it is possible to rebuild these relationships and create a stronger foundation based on acceptance and love. In this chapter, we will explore strategies for healing strained relationships, finding common ground and shared values, allowing time for adjustment and growth, and establishing healthy boundaries.

Healing Strained Relationships

When you come out to your loved ones, it can cause a range of emotions and reactions. Some may respond with immediate acceptance, while others may struggle to understand or express negative sentiments. To heal strained relationships, consider the following steps:

Empathy and Understanding: Understand that your loved ones may need time to process the information and may have deeply ingrained beliefs or biases that they need to confront. Practice empathy and try to see things from their perspective.

Open Communication: Initiate an open and honest dialogue with your loved ones. Express your feelings and experiences, and encourage them to share their thoughts and concerns. This open communication can help bridge the gap and foster understanding.

Seek Mediation if Needed: In some cases, strained relationships may require the assistance of a professional mediator or therapist. A neutral third party can help facilitate discussions, encourage healthy communication, and provide guidance on rebuilding the relationship.

Finding Common Ground And Shared

Values

While it is essential to acknowledge and respect differences in beliefs and values, finding common ground and shared values can help rebuild relationships. Here are some strategies to consider:

Identifying Shared Interests: Explore shared hobbies, activities, or interests that can serve as a common ground. Engaging in these activities together can help foster a sense of connection and remind both parties of the bond they share beyond sexual orientation.

Shared Values and Principles: Focus on identifying shared values and principles that both parties hold dear. Emphasize the importance of love, respect, and acceptance, as these are often universal values that can serve as a foundation for rebuilding relationships.

Education and Awareness: Provide resources and information to your loved ones to help them understand sexual orientation better. Encourage them to educate themselves, ask questions, and challenge any misconceptions they may have. This mutual effort to learn and grow can create a positive environment for rebuilding relationships.

Allowing Time For Adjustment And Growth

Rebuilding relationships takes time, and both parties need to allow each other the space to adjust and grow. Here are some suggestions:

Patience and Compassion: Recognize that adjusting to this new information may take time for your loved ones. Practice patience and compassion while they navigate their feelings and emotions.
Gradual Exposure: For some family and friends, the initial revelation may come as a shock. Gradually expose them to your life and experiences, giving them time to see that your sexual orientation does not change who you are as a person.

Celebrate Progress: Acknowledge and celebrate small steps of acceptance and understanding. This positive reinforcement can encourage continued growth and improvement in the relationship

Establishing Healthy Boundaries

Establishing healthy boundaries is crucial in any relationship, particularly when rebuilding strained ones. Consider the following aspects:

Self-Care: Prioritize your well-being and establish boundaries that protect your mental and emotional health. Communicate your needs clearly and assertively, ensuring that your loved ones understand and respect them.

Mutual Respect: Encourage mutual respect by

setting boundaries that apply to both parties. This includes refraining from making hurtful or derogatory comments, avoiding invasive questions, and maintaining privacy for all involved.

Consistency and Reinforcement: Consistently reinforce the established boundaries and remind your loved ones of the importance of respecting them. This will help create a healthier dynamic in the relationship.

Rebuilding strained relationships after explaining your sexual orientation to family and friends requires patience, understanding, and effective communication. By practicing empathy, finding common ground, allowing time for adjustment and growth, and establishing healthy boundaries, you can create an environment that fosters acceptance and love. Remember, healing takes time, and not all relationships may be salvageable. Focus on nurturing those relationships that show potential for growth and surround yourself with a support system that embraces and accepts you for who you are.

CONCLUSION

Coming out and explaining one's sexual orientation to family and friends is a profoundly personal experience. While it may not always be a smooth or effortless process, it is an essential step towards living a life that is true to oneself. It requires courage and vulnerability, but it is a necessary path towards authenticity and self-acceptance.

Each individual's journey is unique, and there is no right or wrong way to come out. It is a deeply personal decision that should be made on one's own terms and timeline. Some may choose to have individual conversations with loved ones, while others may opt for a more public announcement. Whatever approach is chosen, it is important to remember that honesty and open communication are key.

The road to understanding and acceptance from

family and friends may have its challenges. Some loved ones may struggle to comprehend or accept this new information initially, and it may take time for them to process and adjust. It is essential to approach these conversations with patience, love, and understanding, allowing space for their own emotions and reactions.

Building a supportive network is crucial. Seek out individuals who accept and celebrate your identity, whether they are friends, support groups, or LGBTQ + communities. Surrounding yourself with people who value and embrace you for who you are can provide a sense of belonging and empowerment. Their support can help counterbalance any negative reactions you may encounter, and they can serve as a source of strength during this transformative period.

Remember, you deserve acceptance and respect just as you are. Your sexual orientation is an integral part of your identity, and it is not something to be ashamed of or hidden away. Embrace your true colors and allow yourself to be seen and understood. By living authentically, you pave the way for deeper connections, love, and understanding in your relationships.

Your journey may have its ups and downs, but with time and perseverance, you have the power to shape your own narrative. Stay true to yourself, be patient with others, and remember that your identity is something to be celebrated. By sharing your truth, you not only create an opportunity for personal growth and self-acceptance, but you also contribute to the broader movement of LGBTQ+ visibility and acceptance in society.

Good luck on your journey, and may it lead you to a place of acceptance, happiness, and fulfillment.